The Art of Resolving Differences

By Geri McArdle

Table of Contents

Preface 1

   How Is the Book Organized? 1

   Why Read This Book? 1

Introduction...3

   What Are Your Hot Buttons?...4

   How We Deal with Differences Today...5

   Different People and Behaviors 6

Chapter 1 — Differences Defined 7

   Overview of Differences..8

   Perception versus Reality..8

   Attitude versus Behavior...9

   Attitude Questionnaire 10

   Answer Key..10

   Differences, Deviation, and Cognitive Dissonance 12

      Cognitive Dissonance Between Two Parties...................................14

      Reacting to Dissonance 15

      Best Practices Regarding Dissonance 15

      Quick Self-Appraisal..16

   Differences, Disagreement, and Conflict..17

   Summary 18

Chapter 2 — Power Bases and Differences..19

   Positional Versus Personal Power...20

Power Base Types 22

Stages of Power 24

Power Sources 27

    Power Base Self-Awareness 27

    Power Base Questionnaire 27

    Power Profile 30

Summary 31

Chapter 3 — Exploring Differences 33

Four Sources of Difference 33

    Scenario #1 36

    Scenario #2 36

    Scenario #3 37

Responses to Differences 39

    Avoidance 40

    Diffusion 40

    Confrontation 40

Behavior Arising from Differences 41

    Scenario #1 42

    Scenario #2 42

    Scenario #3 42

    Scenario #4 43

Summary 43

Chapter 4 — Unpacking Differences 45

Pre-Conflict Strategies 45

Pros and Cons of Conflict 47

Responses to Conflicts 48

Elements of Conflict..48

Positive and Negative Aspects of Conflict Exercise 50

Goals and Conflict...50

Negative and Positive Outcomes of Conflict 51

Win-Lose, Lose-Lose, or Win-Win...52

Summary 53

Chapter 5 — Managing Differences..55

Identifying Styles of Managing Differences...................................55

Managing Differences Styles Questionnaire 56

Style Descriptors 57

Your Score 59

Managing Behavior..60

Guiding Effective Collaborative Behavior 61

Conflict Style Action Plan 63

Summary 64

Chapter 6 — The Intricacies of Managing Differences....................65

Four Skills...65

Diagnose..66

Initiate...66

Listen 66

Problem Solve 67

Signals and Emotions..68

Dealing with Emotional Situations 68

Negotiating to Win... 69

Negotiating Persuasively 69

Negotiating Effectively.. 70

Summary 72

Conclusion 73

Preface

Conflict is all around us. It can make us feel uncomfortable, sometimes scared or helpless. *The Art of Resolving Differences* is based on 30 years of consultation, research, seminars, and teaching with audiences and organizations of all kinds.

This book is not another book about conflict; it's about using your wisdom and logic to resolve difficult situations. Start today to take control of yourself and manage the difficult situations that you face each day.

How Is the Book Organized?

- Chapter 1 defines the term "difference" and explains how our perception of reality can affect our behavior and attitude about others and situations.
- Chapter 2 identifies your power base.
- Chapter 3 discusses the link that exists between our power base and our behavior maturity.
- Chapter 4 takes you through a self-assessment survey to help you understand the decisions you make when in a problem situation.
- Chapter 5 provides tools you need to manage differences.
- Finally, chapter 6 discusses some of the intricacies that can emerge when managing a difference.

Why Read This Book?

The initial publication appeared in 1995. The book has changed a lot—presenting new self-assessment inventories, instructive case studies, and diagnostics that you can apply immediately. Take two hours, read the book, and tomorrow you will be a different person—I guarantee it!

Introduction

Most of us have found ourselves in a difficult situation that ultimately resulted in a heated debate filled with over-charged emotions evolving around different points of view. Or, we have witnessed a conflict between two others. From an objective perspective, you could see that a resolution was feasible—if the two parties could find a way to see the other's point of view.

From your perspective, you could identify where or when the two parties were coming from. In addition, it was easier to see who may have been at fault or played a bigger role in the escalation of the issue than the participants were willing to see or admit.

Even though you could see that the keys to resolving the issue were within reach, when these highly charged situations escalate, for the people engaged in dispute, they often feel impossible to resolve. Everyone has witnessed or been involved in a situation like this. It is a natural result of human interaction.

Interpersonal interactions have the potential to develop and evolve in either desirable or undesirable ways. When interpersonal interactions take a negative turn, they can range from low level conflicts such as discourse, disagreements, and debates, to scenarios of a more serious nature like verbal abuse or physical violence.

Regardless of the degree and development of the interpersonal conflict, it all stems simply from differences. Some differences tend to evoke conflict or friction between opposing parties more than others.

Many hot-button subjects can escalate emotions during discussion. Here are some common examples:

Human Rights	Lifestyle Choices	Child Raising
Ethics	Sexuality	Workplace Cooperation
Religion	Money	Politics

Topics such as these can create friction no matter how close the parties may be. It is human nature to find yourself worked up in a discussion when you feel passionate about your point of view.

What Are Your Hot Buttons?

Are you someone who is more reserved, cordial, and diplomatic around people with whom you are less familiar, i.e., co-workers, acquaintances, and strangers? Yet, you seem to experience more heated discussions or conflict with those with whom you are closest, i.e., friends, family, spouses, and roommates?

Maybe the *opposite* is true for you instead: Do you get along well and experience a healthy form of discussion with your inner circle, despite a difference in opinion? Yet when you share opposing thoughts with someone you aren't familiar with or don't respect as deeply, do your highly charged emotions get the better of you?

In either case, do you find yourself on one side of an argument, and regardless of how you try to explain your viewpoint, the other party doesn't get you or your point of view, and nothing is ever truly resolved?

Guess what? If you answered "yes," you are not alone!

Keep in mind that no matter what type of person you are, or how you conduct yourself during your interactions with others, *no one is immune from conflict.*

There is a great, big world out there full of narcissists who shamelessly steal recognition from others, entitled slackers, unappreciative takers, passive-aggressive personalities, gossipers, and countless other jerks who live, work, worship, and drive in your world. Beyond those draining, stress-inducers who you wish you could deport to a desert island, conflict can also arise with the people you respect and love.

Perhaps you may even discover that some people who you once categorized in the "jerk" list have more value than you initially thought. It is not uncommon for so-called foes to evolve into friends and for relationships in all stages and of all kinds to repair and thrive.

All discussion—the good, the bad, and the ugly—stems from our differences. To be different should not be viewed negatively, although it often is viewed that way. What makes us different is what makes us individuals. Differences should be welcomed and celebrated.

When differences cause friction, this too should be celebrated as an opportunity. The goal is to become aware of these touchy, awkward, tense interactions, and disagreements; that way, they can be used to create solutions that bring value to all parties. By changing our perspective about differences, we can take time to reframe how we see the situation and consider how this circumstance can benefit the parties involved.

How We Deal with Differences Today

It is not uncommon to experience conflict with another individual and for things to continue or escalate without the parties ever reaching an outcome that benefits everybody. Let's face it, passive-aggressive behavior is the norm of the day. The electronic age we now live in robs us of opportunities to practice our social skills. In the workplace, as well as at home or in other social structures, conflicts occur. However, instead of addressing the issue with the goal of solving the problem, the two parties stay stagnant in their state of disagreement. They may also use outlets like social media to air their issues and solicit biased feedback from their followers. Or they may go to other people in their circle of influence and badmouth the person they are quarrelling with. Yet another method may be to simply dismiss responsibility from the problem by withdrawing from the person. None of these options produce healthy outcomes.

Yet, all it takes to resolve differences is a flexible set of eyes and an open mind.

Different People and Behaviors

People are defined by their behaviors. Your reality is made up entirely from your perception. The keys to a successful outcome are in understanding how differences can manifest themselves in any given situation and preparing yourself to handle them so they don't escalate into an unmanageable conflict.

This book discusses a wide range of factors that come into play when you attempt to manage differences. You can expect to acquire an understanding of the factors motivating individuals when they encounter differences. After reading this book, answering the questions, and working through the exercises it contains, you will never again have to walk away from a confrontational situation feeling that you were unable to air your differences constructively. Remember, no matter our differences, things can turn out okay.

Through mastering our understanding of what makes us different from others, we have the precious ability to grow as individuals, as well as in our relationships with the other party.

Chapter 1 — Differences Defined

Chapter 1 begins with the definition of "difference" and continues to explain that differences are based on our perception of reality. It further explains that differences, if not managed, can evolve into conflict. The chapter ends with a discussion and provides examples of the three types of conflict situations.

There are many definitions of difference. The following are the two most appropriate to this book.

- Difference: a point or way in which people or things are not the same.
- Differences [plural]: disagreements about something

Differences can become apparent and a source of conflict when people struggle as they share their preferences, ideas, perceptions, or goals. At some time, you will encounter people who hold views and act in ways that are different from your own.

In the generations during and after the Great Depression in the United States, people were all displaced. They coped as kids and young adults by bonding together to make everything work. Being poor was the norm. They moved in together and stepped up for their kids, and most, when starting their careers as young adults, became public servants, working for the government, nonprofits, or community.

I am a "boomer." Traditionally, we took time to manage differences that caused conflict. In the 1950s and 1960s (my generation), civility and integrity ruled.

In today's hyper-speed world, proactive strategies are required, and sometimes integrity and honesty (and lack thereof) are blamed on demands and a person's distorted reality.

Overview of Differences

What are differences? Differences are based on perceptions of your own reality. A difference is a point or way in which people or things are not the same. Differences can become apparent when people share their preferences, ideas, perceptions, biases, goals, and culture.

Differences can evolve into disagreements, which can ultimately result in one of the three types of conflict:

1. Overt: a conflict that involves an open and adversarial interaction.
2. Escalated: a conflict that occurs when groups with different power levels disagree.
3. Covert: a conflict that involves societal differences such as gender, race, or religion.

Perception versus Reality

Most of us consistently seek to establish predictable behavior patterns. These behavioral patterns build networks with other people, places, and things. The relationships help each of us as we make connections and also make sense of every experience.

Your reaction and how you interact with others are based upon the way you perceive the world around you, and your interpretation of reality provides you with a unique viewpoint. This viewpoint is affected by learned childhood patterns of behavior.

To manage differences, you must first understand how you feel about them. Our natural inclination is to assume that our way is the best. You may have fixed thoughts, perceptions, or attitudes about differences, which influence the role you play when one arises. Differences become apparent when values, priorities, and goals seem incompatible. Such differences are frequently based on an individual's perceptions rather than on reality.

Every day, you interpret events and use a system of beliefs based on your childhood, background, and experiences. Your beliefs support your reality and create meaning out of otherwise random events, while they influence your thoughts, actions, and reactions. You also access folk wisdom (stories or truisms) passed down through your family and personal theories that help to influence and guide your reality. Beliefs, ideas, and values taught to you as children are the building blocks for your perceptions and values.

Take the example of beauty, specifically feminine beauty in our culture and others. Standards of feminine beauty vary across cultures. In one culture and time period, tanned skin was a sign that someone was a laborer or a peasant forced to work in the sun. However, fair skin was a sign of affluence, proof that you were not a peasant. Today, we see tanned skin as a sign of healthy color or a person who is affluent enough to take vacations and spend time outdoors, whereas we view pale skin as unhealthy. However, people can possess health, affluence, and beauty regardless of their skin pigment.

Attitude versus Behavior

Your perception of reality profoundly influences attitude and behavior. Attitude is an individual's habitual outlook on the world. It significantly determines how you choose to conduct yourself in given situations, including those characterized by differences of opinion. That is, attitude guides behavior. Behavior is how you choose to conduct yourself—both at home and in the workplace.

Look at the 10 commonly held beliefs about differing viewpoints in the questionnaire. Remember, while management is administrative, leadership is inspirational. Leadership focuses on what must be done to ensure that the organization and the staff succeed. With today's workplace comes diversity. Diverse cultures in the workplace are positive and must be acknowledged and respected.

Attitude Questionnaire

Directions: To help you identify your basic beliefs about differences, look at these 10 commonly held beliefs about differing viewpoints. Read each statement carefully. Indicate how you feel about the statement; mark a plus for *agree* and a minus for *disagree.*

1. ___ Once I get engaged in a heated discussion about differences, I just can't stop.

2. ___ If people communicated more, there would be fewer differences.

3. ___ There is always a winner and a loser when matters of difference are expressed.

4. ___ Differing viewpoints are something I want to avoid.

5. ___ When I get upset, I shouldn't discuss my differences about important issues.

6. ___ Differences in viewpoint make me feel uneasy and anxious.

7. ___ I like to win when differences present a challenge.

8. ___ It is difficult for me to discuss my feelings when I might have a difference with colleagues, friends, or family members.

9. ___ I can seldom think straight when my opinions are different from others.

10. ___ Resolving differences has provided great opportunities for my personal growth.

*Answer **Key***

Since your answers are based on your attitudes, there are no right or wrong answers to this questionnaire. You're entitled to your feelings, attitudes, and beliefs. The following suggestions will help you understand your answers:

1. Most of us have difficulty thinking logically and fairly during a heated discussion.

    Yet, it is important to take time to think through our responses. Picture yourself in the other person's shoes: What is he or she thinking, feeling, sensing, hearing, and believing? Get a different perspective.

2. Do more listening than talking. You can't think and talk at the same time. This is especially true when you try to understand another's point of view to resolve differences.

3. Differences of opinion don't have to become win-lose situations. Consider redefining the issues by noting points of compatibility or congruity. Acknowledge when the other party makes a point that you agree with or understand. This helps to improve your opportunities to reach amenable terms, and you both can win.

4. You will never be able to wish away or avoid your differences; learn to deal with them. Problems can be swept under the rug temporarily, but they always find a way to resurface and fester.

5. You should discuss your differences. Silence does not make problems go away. The silent treatment does not help the other person understand your differences. Address the issue as soon as you find an opportunity for all parties involved to speak in a constructive environment.

6. It's normal to feel uneasy. Be bold—dare to take charge! The relief you will feel when the issue is resolved will outweigh the anxiety that will burden you while the issue remains unresolved.

7. Winning is not the goal—it's how skillfully you manage the difference.

8. In matters of difference, emotions make communicating difficult for everyone involved. It is hard to express yourself clearly and to listen with an open mind. Be mindful of your breathing during these discussions. This will keep your emotions at bay and provide a space of awareness for you to concentrate on listening over speaking.

9. Sometimes you lose your thoughts. When it happens, stop and ask for clarification of the issue or problem. Determine your own needs and identify those of the other party. Use the new information as the key to rephrase your dialogue, to unlock the doors to your differences.

10. We often hear that problems create opportunities. When you encounter a problem, take time out and think about at least one alternative way to resolve your differences. You'll be surprised at the flexibility you can exercise!

Differences, Deviation, and Cognitive Dissonance

You may have noticed that the route you need to take to satisfy your needs sometimes leads to further differences, deviation, and cognitive dissonance. Every member of society has a specific viewpoint. Our varying viewpoints in turn create a world of differences, which we need to respect. Some differences, for example, follow definite patterns and are not typically associated with angry feelings; other differences involve irrational behavior and lead to disruptive and even violent actions.

Here are two examples of different approaches to similar problems. One behavior pattern does not lead to angry feelings and the other does:

- A college-student, Mark, who experiences anxiety for being late to class may choose to get up hours early to ensure he makes it on time.

- Mary, who also feels pressured by being late, may choose to speed, run a red light or stop sign, illegally park her car in a closer spot, or get in a fistfight with someone she carelessly runs into in the walkway. All of these behaviors are examples of irrational, disruptive, and even violent actions Mary makes to get to class on time.

Differences become apparent in contrast to some agreed-upon standard or norm of behavior. When there are many people gathered to purchase the newest version of a smartphone, the norm is that the first person to arrive is serviced first, and everyone falls in line as they arrive. A line will naturally form among people without any particular person coordinating it.

Deviations, however, account for differences that appear occasionally, which are inconsistent with one of society's established behavioral norms. Paul may bypass the line and insist on being serviced by the store associate first simply because he feels he is a superior customer. That is a deviation.

Obstructionist motives and unsuccessful attempts to resolve interpersonal issues may surface when a person behaves irrationally in an uncomfortable situation.

An example of an alternative motive would be for Judy to barge toward the front of the line and demand to speak to an associate. To the others in line, Judy's actions are irrational and unjustified, but perhaps Judy wants to inform someone that headlights have been left on in a vehicle in the parking lot.

The difference between Paul and Judy is that Judy would not have barged to the front of the line without a reason that justified her stepping outside the norm. Paul's belief that he has more value as a customer than others, insisting that he be serviced before others who arrived before him, is evidence of Paul's cognitive dissonance.

Cognitive dissonance describes times when it becomes difficult or impossible for an individual to reconcile perceptions and reality. The individual may notice feelings of tension or anxiety. While conflicting feelings are part of an internal process that others may not notice, the feelings may result in behaviors others find confusing.

Let's also keep in mind that Paul's cognitive dissonance stems from the fact that as a child, he battled a life-threatening condition. As a result, Paul's parents put his needs before his siblings' whether they were big or small, so Paul grew up believing that what he needed and wanted came first. This belief has bled beyond his status in his household and into his perception of his place in society as well.

Cognitive Dissonance Between Two Parties

In another example, cognitive dissonance can also arise when two people who meet or work on a project together have dramatically different perceptions or feelings about an issue. The collision of incompatible views creates tension that ultimately must be resolved by modifying one viewpoint.

Two nursing interns are assigned to two patients involved in a drunk-driving accident. One patient is the guilty driver and the other an innocent pedestrian. The doctor orders the interns, Amy and Beth, to monitor the pain of both patients and administer pain killers based on how the patients describe their pain levels.

Amy and Beth meet the pedestrian, Cami, a 16-year-old soccer player whose knee is broken. Cami describes her pain level as a 7 out of 10. Amy gives her 75% of the maximum dose to Cami for her pain, per protocol.

Beth asks the drunk driver, Daniel, about the level of pain he is experiencing from fractured ribs. Daniel describes his pain as a 7 out of 10. Beth deviates from the protocol, giving him only the minimum for his pain, with the mindset that he caused his own injuries as well as Cami's injuries.

In this case, the societal norm is to treat both patients equally. Beth has deviated from the norm by giving Daniel less than she would have given Cami. Beth's choice is evidence that she has cognitive dissonance regarding the standard of ethics and care upheld by the hospital.

Amy discovers Beth's decision to withhold the standard dose from Daniel and confronts her about her action. Beth is surprised that Amy doesn't share her viewpoint regardless of the hospital rules. Now the two interns are experiencing cognitive dissonance between them as a team.

Reacting to Dissonance

When we feel the tension that develops because of dissonance, we can either change our behavior or change the way we view the situation. To cope, we make compromises that we feel will benefit and balance the relationships that can be jeopardized by dissonance.

In the nursing example, Beth wants to ease the tension between her and Amy. Beth wants Amy to recognize that despite her harsh judgment of Daniel, Beth is still a passionate and caring nurse. For the next few days, Beth volunteers for the more difficult patients and assignments, making Amy's job easier whenever she can. Beth has modified her behavior even though she feels no remorse about her decision. Amy appreciates how Beth has stepped up and volunteered, but Amy doesn't feel better about Beth's choice to treat Daniel differently.

When Daniel's six-year-old daughter, Ellie, visits him, Beth's viewpoint on the situation changes. Ellie is distraught to see her father with cuts, bruises, casts, and medicine lines coming from his body. She is sad that her daddy is in pain and scared that he is going to die. Beth's compassion for the child helps Beth see that her place is to care for patients, not judge them. Beth sincerely promises Ellie that she will take good care of her daddy, and Beth continues to be as attentive and ethical with his care as she is with other patients.

Best Practices Regarding Dissonance

People who know how to cope well with dissonance may behave in a more constructive manner (e.g., going to the gym, running, or engaging in some other kind of physical activity). In this way, they redirect their focus harmlessly away from the person(s) or subject(s) of the differences.

Recognize that not all differences, deviations, and feelings of dissonance are negative experiences. Similarly, not all differences result in a conflict. Differences become potential sources of conflict or distress only when not properly addressed.

Quick Self-Appraisal

Have you ever experienced differences that centered around one or more of the following issues?

- Pressure to meet deadlines
- Personal differences
- Distribution of resources
- Authority
- Seniority
- Dispute settlement
- Affirmative action
- Interdepartmental concerns
- Use of human resources
- Giving and receiving information

Don't judge yourself harshly if you answered "yes" to any of these issues. Instead, ask yourself why the differences reached the point they did. Take the opportunity to learn how you can deal with differences and take control of your options now.

Differences, Disagreement, and Conflict

Differences in attitude, perceptions, and behaviors can result in conflict. When differences become a disagreement, this disagreement, if not managed, can become a conflict situation.

Overt conflict involves open, adversarial interaction. The interaction can range from mild disagreement to high-level disagreement that results in fighting. Labor-management disputes that make headlines are typical examples of overt conflict.

Escalated conflict occurs when groups with different levels of power enter into a disagreement. An example of this can be seen in an intergroup meeting between a low-power group and a high-power group. Perceiving their vulnerability, the low-power group may feel forced to withhold information from the high-power group. Without the information, the high-power group would be unaware that the low-power group is dissatisfied with specific issues. Over time, the low-power group would continue to repress information to avoid repercussions. Such differences are harmful; they deny opportunities to discuss and resolve the problem and to work toward positive, valuable solutions.

For example a group of new hires (the low-power group) at a marketing company witnessed people writing hurtful jokes on the refrigerator in the break area. The high-power group is composed of the owners of the company. The owners' son, Brian, who works at the company, may be involved in the jokes. The low-power group hesitates to speak up about the jokes because they fear the consequences. If Brian is innocent, he may still get in trouble with his parents. If he is part of the jokes, his parents may not respond appropriately. By the low-power group choosing not to bring up the issue, the owners are unaware of the offensive problem and cannot correct it, regardless of who was involved.

Covert conflict often involves societal differences such as gender, race, and religious discrimination. These differences are highly sensitive and must be handled with extra care and consideration. Laws and business regulations that guarantee equal opportunity can do little to change deep-seated attitudes and behaviors.

Consequently, interpersonal differences can turn into conflict unless a catalyst—an unbiased person or set of circumstances—successfully motivates a discussion where differences can be aired openly and freely.

Summary

Differences in attitudes, perceptions, and behaviors can result in conflict. And when differences become disagreements, overt, escalated, and covert conflict can evolve.

These three types of conflict couldn't occur; however, without one key ingredient: power. As you'll learn in chapter 2, power is the underlying issue in the majority of conflicts based on differences that we must handle. It is the driving force in many adversarial situations. You will see that power is a multidimensional agent, derived from various bases and sources. It plays a number of roles in matters where differences are at issue.

Chapter 2 — Power Bases and Differences

Chapter 2 discusses the various power bases and how we affect something or someone when using them. It further discusses the relationship between power and conflict. The chapter concludes with an opportunity to complete a self-assessment inventory to help you identify your primary and secondary power bases.

The decision-making process is a key element in managing differences. Your decision-making process, your perspective of difference, and your source of power are all intertwined concepts that influence conflict.

Part of the learning process is to define your power base and analyze your choices during the decision-making process.

Power has many definitions. At the simplest level, power is the ability to do or to affect something or someone. Power handled wisely at an organizational level can inspire actions that set a good example for others to follow and provide the leadership that prevents differences from becoming destructive.

Definition: Power is an individual's potential to influence.

Most conflict that results from difference is an underlying issue of power. Differences, which have the potential to escalate into destructive conflicts, usually involve the issue of power. One party has power while the other party doesn't; one party feels abused, doesn't know how to wield power; one party doesn't want power or wishes to have more.

Differences can lead to struggles and useless conflict about power—both with others and with oneself. In a variety of situations, understanding power is the key to managing behavior and productively resolving differences.

Positional Versus Personal Power

Power takes on two forms: positional and personal. An individual who induces compliance from others because of his or her status within an organization has positional power. A person with influence derived from personality, gender, race, education, and behavior is said to have personal power. All individuals possess some form of power to one degree or another, and most have varying levels of power among different groups within their personal and professional circles.

Another way to think about positional power is the power that has been appointed to someone, whereas personal power is more organic.

For example: If you are a producer at a radio station, you have genuine organizational (i.e., positional) power over your immediate staff: DJs, administration, tech crew, etc. At the same time, you defer to senior executives and the owners. In this sense, you have limited positional power. Let's say that you arrange to have a guest musician, a heart-throb guitarist, visit the studio to plug his upcoming concert tour. While the guitarist doesn't own the radio station, everyone in the building, including the executives and owner, will most likely cater to his every whim to make his experience at the station exceptional. The guitarist has personal power. He might demand hard-to-find treats for his dressing room, insist that his coffee be served at exactly 125 degrees, or request that someone from the station walk and clean up after his dogs during his visit, and everyone will bend over backward to meet his requests.

Positional and personal power are two important elements related to the way we view differences. Both are crucial to understanding what motivates you and others when differences arise.

The following basic concepts relate to power:

1. Power is finite to resolving differences and should not be perceived in a negative light.

Many social scientists maintain that leadership and power form a symbiotic relationship between the two. Let's look at how power is used in our work and personal relationships. Power holds the potential for influence. In this sense, power becomes a valuable resource that you may choose to use when seeking to resolve differences.

A distinction should be drawn between leadership and power. Leadership, in the broadest sense, is your ability to influence another individual, while power is the influence potential of a leader. (Note: you do not have to hold a position of authority in an organization to act as a leader; remember this point with each action you make or word you speak.)

If power is defined as potential to influence, how do you distinguish between power and authority? Authority is a distinct type of power that finds its base by default (i.e., the individual's formal role within an organization).

2. Power is the central component of difference.

Power can be a matter of perception. Some differences in power are real, while perceptions create others. The chief executive officer of a company has authoritative (i.e., positional) power over a department manager. In another example, because of his gender, one supervisor is perceived by his female colleagues as being more powerful.

3. You have one or more power bases.

We derive power from a variety of sources or bases. Some of these sources lie within the individual. (e.g., "I'm more mature than the others.") Other power bases are dependent on the individual's position in the organizational hierarchy (e.g. "I'm the department manager."), his or her expertise (e.g. "I'm more experienced in this area than anyone else."), or how others perceive that individual's expertise. (e.g. "She sure knows what she's doing; just by watching her management style with her co-workers and subordinates, it's clear why they brought her in to make the department profitable again.")

4. Power bases can shift based on matters of difference.

A competent manager can become ineffective if her assistant successfully undermines her authority; in this case, the assistant would be perceived as having more power than the manager. A seasoned (older) assistant may have more power than a newly appointed (younger) manager. If you called a meeting, you might have power because you initiated it; however, be mindful of the power bases or positions that exist.

Power Base Types

Once we understand the sources of our power, we can be more selective as to when we choose to enact our power bases. Let's look at six power bases.

1. **Coercive power** is based on fear. If you exert coercive power, you can induce compliance through the understanding that the other person's failure to comply will lead to his or her punishment, to retaliation, or ultimately to dismissal. For the most part, someone exercising coercive power is not concerned with whether his issue is compatible with another person's issue. In other words, to use coercive power on another is a statement that you have no concern for the needs of the other party.

2. **Connection power** is based on an individual's personal or professional connection with influential or important people within or outside an organization.

3. **Reward power** is based on an individual's ability to reward others who believe that they will gain opportunities for growth within an organization (e.g., recognition, pay raise, or promotion) by complying.

4. **Legitimate power** is based on an individual's authoritative position. The higher their position, the broader others will perceive the scope of their legitimate power. If you have a high degree of legitimate power, you can induce compliance or influence others, simply based upon your position within the organization. In such cases, unfortunately, the subordinates' viewpoints and differences of opinion often go unrecognized and unattended.

5. **Referent power** is based on personal traits and characteristics. An individual who possesses referent power is generally well-liked and admired by others because of his or her personality.

6. **Expert power** is based on education, knowledge, or possession of expertise or skills that, through respect, influence others. An individual with expert power is perceived as possessing the expertise required to complete a particular task.

Which type of power base is best for minimizing differences that may arise? In studies conducted by a number of social scientists, expert and referent power achieved the highest levels of satisfactory performance on the job.

Legitimate, reward, and coercive power are organizationally determined and designed to be equal for supervisors at a hierarchical level. They are bases for compliance—not satisfaction. Ultimately, your power base and how you choose to resolve differences will be vastly affected by the specific circumstances of the situation.

Think for a minute about each of these six power bases, and try to think of a situation where you used these power sources to influence you to take action. Can you also think of some scenarios where you used these on others?

While some individuals start with little power and gradually build and develop power sources, others gradually allow their power sources to erode. The perception others hold about an individual's power provides that individual with the ability to influence others' behavior, induce compliance, or persuade others to agree with a point of view.

Stages of Power

According to David McClelland, an American psychology theorist who was the founder of Need Theory and a faculty member at Harvard University from 1956 to 1998, there are four distinct stages in the development of individual power. Each stage represents a higher level of maturity regarding a person's need for power.

Stage I (Low Maturity Level). This stage involves incorporating power from a source outside the individual. Early in life, this strength comes from parents, then from friends, a spouse, or an admired leader or mentor. By experiencing or sharing the power of a strong person, the individual feels empowered, which leads him or her to falsely believe that anyone can be persuaded easily to abandon his or her differences and take on the beliefs, traits, and actions of the individual.

For example Jackie had worked in restaurants since she was 12 years old. By the time she was 24, she had held every position from busser to bartender and server to administration and training. When moved to a new town, she took an entry-level opportunity as a restaurant manager at a new restaurant concept. She believed she held the experience and the supportive personality it took to manage staff through leadership. Yet, she was surprised to find that regardless of her experience and work ethic, she had no real leadership power with the new restaurant staff. Many employees felt that she would be ineffective because of her young age.

Her first step in becoming a self-sufficient manager was to shadow the current general manager as she trained in various roles. The staff acted respectfully to Jackie's position while in the presence of other managers. Still, they did not respond positively or constructively when Jackie attempted to uphold the standards of the restaurant on her own. Though Jackie tried hard to prove herself in her knowledge, willingness to be a team player, and ability to give excellent service, the staff continued to undermine her authority. Jackie felt it was necessary to address these issues with the general manager and the employees through a conversation. Jackie thought that the general manager could make the employees treat her with more respect, but the conversations proved useless. Only time would build relationships with the staff.

Stage II (Moderate Maturity Level). This stage is independent of the self. Usually, when an individual learns self-control, a powerful feeling occurs.

For example: In a few months, Jackie successfully started working shifts on her own. She still had hope that the staff could be won over and realize that she wanted to be a manager for the right reasons, not just to wield power. She used some of her perks as a manager, like a nightly free meal, to reward and recognize staff members who were doing a good job. She also liked wearing her swipe card and her keys so that they were visible to others and would remind them that she was the leader. Some employees were starting to turn to her regarding issues with other managers, and Jackie began to think she could take actions that would bring her closer to the acceptance of the staff.

Stage III (Moderate to Rather High Maturity Level). While the primary form of behavior in this stage is competitive, helping behavior is also manifested (i.e., the decision-making process).

For example: After several months pass, Jackie's effectiveness as a manager increases. She feels confident in her ability to solve problems in the restaurant, whether it is among staff or with customers. A new position with additional responsibility becomes available, which could mean an increased salary for Jackie. However, she is not the only manager who would like the promotion. Jackie sees opportunities to compete with the other managers and resists the temptation to point out their inadequacies to prove she's got more know-how in the restaurant. She sees opportunities to prove her worthiness for the role by teaching newer managers and the ones vying for the promotion, some of her most helpful tips.

Stage IV (High Maturity Level). Power derived from a higher authority (i.e., legitimate power) is the final stage in which power is exerted in conformance with duty. At this stage, power is socialized and institutionalized at the highest level. The individual has successfully integrated the three previous stages into the legitimate power and can use all stages effectively to address and resolve differences that might arise.

For example Jackie wanted the promotion badly enough to come to work early, as well as stay late. Jackie took it upon herself to identify areas of the restaurant that needed improvement by soliciting feedback from employees and customers. She took the initiative to resolve issues and innovate better methods for running the store. Every day she made sure she asked an employee how she could help them and tried to get to know them on a more personal level. Jackie tried to be the first to recognize when she had made an error and stayed consistent with the standards of the company. She tried to put herself in the shoes of the guest or the employee when things went wrong and problems arose. Jackie convinced the owners that she was the best suited for the promotion, and the employees who once resisted Jackie's leadership were happy, she was appointed to the role.

Think about the following two questions. Once you answer the questions, think through the challenging issues you face and what you do differently.

1. What are some examples from your experience of good use of power in resolving differences? Identify what made them so.

2. What are some examples from your own experience of bad use of power in resolving differences? Identify what made them so.

Power Sources

Although the six bases can be used to resolve differences, induce compliance, or influence the behavior of an individual or group, power can vary greatly. Part of the variance in power is due to the organization for which an individual works and his or her rank within the organization (i.e., position power). The rest of the variance is due to individual differences with other types of power (i.e., personal power). The vehicle that you choose to resolve a difference in the six bases is the key to a productive resolution of differences.

Power Base Self-Awareness

Directions: Think about how you handle power. Review the six types of power, and think about how you use each of the sources to resolve situations involving differences.

1. Coercive Power _______________________________

2. Legitimate Power _______________________________

3. Expert Power _______________________________

4. Reward Power _______________________________

5. Referent Power _______________________________

6. Connection Power _______________________________

Power Base Questionnaire

Directions: Think of a goal you would like to accomplish that you cannot do unless you resolve differences between yourself and another person, "N." Read the following statements and record how helpful each power base would be in assisting you in influencing the behavior of another person to achieve your goal. Use the following scale:

0 = Cannot help me at all achieve my goal

1 = Could possibly help me achieve my goal

2 = Would help me somewhat in achieving my goal

3 = Could definitely help me achieve my goal

_____1. Despite our difference, I want to offer N something I know N wants or values.

_____2. I'm in a position to have someone, whose credentials/relationship N respects, act on my behalf to reconcile the differences between N and myself.

_____3. I can help N achieve his/her goal, despite our differences.

_____4. Using our differences constructively, I can create a situation that would enable me to get what I want from N.

_____5. Despite our differences, I can influence N through my actions.

_____6. Because of our differences, I can convince someone else to hurt, punish, or deprive N.

_____7. By stating our differences clearly, I can make N recognize that we have a lot in common.

_____8. Although differences exist, I can drop names that impress N.

_____9. I can use my professional knowledge and skills with N in areas that will help me achieve my goal.

_____10. I can use persuasive techniques to convince N to drop his or her difference.

_____11. To accomplish my goal, I can negate any existing differences by influencing someone else to give N what he or she wants.

_____12. I can use friendship as a means to resolve any differences between N and myself.

_____13. Despite our differences, I can impress N through the people I know.

_____14. I can get a friend of N's to help resolve our differences to act on my behalf.

_____15. To resolve our differences, I can get someone else who is well connected to influence N.

_____16. I can use N's respect for my education to gain N's support.

_____17. Based on my knowledge in a certain area, I can ask directly for what I want, knowing that N will think it appropriate for me to make the request.

_____18. Recognizing that our differences are being ignored, I can get someone else, who has a legitimate right to ask for something I want, to request what I need from N.

Now, record your answers from your Power Base Questionnaire on the appropriate lines below.

Formal Power

Reward Power	Coercive Power	Legitimate Power
1_____	2_____	3_____
4_____	6_____	17_____
11_____	10_____	18_____
Total_____	Total_____	Total_____

Informal Power

Expert Power	Referent Power	Connection Power
5_____	7_____	8_____
9_____	12_____	13_____
16_____	14_____	15_____
Total_____	Total_____	Total_____

Total your scores for each power base column. The highest scored category indicates your primary power base; the second scored category indicates your secondary power base.

You'll notice that formal and informal power bases are clustered. Formal power bases are seen in more structured situations (e.g., the workplace), where they are more than likely imposed upon the individual. In contrast, the informal power bases tend to be less structured and are more likely filled with self-driven behaviors.

Power Profile

Directions: Read the four statements, and insert your appropriate score. Review your scores. Think about how you answered each statement. What would you do differently, and why? Do you find your score a surprise, or does the score reflect the techniques you use accurately when resolving differences?

1. My formal power base for resolving differences: ______

2. My informal power base for resolving differences: ______

3. The characteristics of both my power bases and the way in which I resolve differences are: ____

4. My method for applying my power bases and resolving differences when confronted with differing opinions: ____

Now, repeat the power profile. This time, respond the way the individual with whom you work closest with would answer. After you have completed this exercise, consider asking that individual to complete the profile. Then, compare your answers and note the amount of difference between your perceptions. Keep in mind that each person's perception is that individual's reality and forms the basis of his or her action.

Summary

No single style determines whether you are maximizing your source of power or decision-making processes related to differences. What is important is that an individual who tries to influence a group uses the appropriate power base to define his or her leadership.

In today's ever-changing and evolutionary approach to management, many organizations have moved away from reliance on power bases that emphasize forced compliance. These organizations have moved toward the use and integration of power bases, which will exert cooperative influence over others. Their intention is to enable individuals to speak up without fear of expressing their differences.

Chapter 3 — Exploring Differences

Chapter 3 discusses how conflicts may arise when differences are not acknowledged, dealt with, and resolved. Specifically, the material examines the behavior pattern that people exhibit when differences arise and provides ways for you to manage the situations to reach a satisfactory resolution.

Personal traits and characteristics are developed early on in life. As we grow and mature, we develop conditioned responses or habit patterns to numerous stimuli. We take many of our actions for granted so that they almost become mechanical. Others perceive the sum total of patterns as personality.

Some behaviors are easily adjusted, while others seem almost impossible to change. Often, the type of difference or one's maturity level determines how easy it is to adjust.

The following four examples of differences are listed in the order of difficulty to resolve, from least difficult (i.e., facts and information) to most difficult (i.e., those issues that surround our systems of values and beliefs).

Four Sources of Difference

1. Facts and Information

   When differences of information or facts are at issue, two parties can see the same facts differently or can disagree on what the facts are. This is the easiest level to manage because it can usually be resolved by sharing information or producing more reliable data.

2. Methods

   This level presumes there is an agreed-upon common goal. Disagreements are about which strategies will be used to reach the goal(s) or about how to approach accomplishing a task. Differences concerning methods assume that there is a common goal, so the differences can usually be resolved by defining a mutually acceptable strategy to reach the goal. While method differences are relatively easy to manage, they are more challenging to resolve than differences concerning facts and information.

3. Goals

    Here, differences occur with regard to achieving specific outcomes in basic goals. Disagreements often center on what should be done, what the focus is, what the common direction is, or whether there is a shared purpose. Collaboration (working together to agree on goals), negotiations, and resolution skills can help to resolve the differences. Because all of the above elements are required to resolve differences, this level is more difficult to manage than the previous two.

4. Values

    This is usually the most difficult level of difference to resolve. While the other levels deal with tangibles, value differences deal with ideology, basic principles, and beliefs. People identify strongly with their values and can be very resistant to change them. The issue becomes whether it is possible to work out a satisfactory outcome without one or the other party compromising their values. This requires a sensitive understanding and respect for each person's values, plus hard work to reach a win-win solution.

Differences may be difficult to resolve because each party may approach the issues from any one of four levels. Also, as differences develop, they may start at one level and shift to a different one. A dialogue that begins with a statement of difference will never move on to the issues of agreement. To stabilize the levels, the parties must establish points of agreement before they state issues of disagreement.

Four Sources of Differences

Facts	Methods	Goals	Values
Easy to resolve			Difficult to resolve

Notice that facts and values are extreme opposites as sources of difference. Differences that move further from informational disputes and closer to disputes over perception or value become increasingly difficult to resolve.

1. What situation would be most difficult for you to resolve?
2. Reviewing the complexity of the difference, which level would be the easiest for you to deal with?

Let's look at some scenarios and identify the source of the difference for each one. Read each scenario. Make note of your thought process. Analyze how you arrived at your final situation decision.

Scenario #1

John and his co-worker, Amanda, have been meeting for several weeks to develop departmental guidelines. During the course of the project, many differences have become apparent, and John has become very uncomfortable working with Amanda.

Two weeks ago, when Amanda rejected his ideas, John felt Amanda wasn't taking him seriously. Apart from the fact that his ideas were dismissed, his feelings were hurt. As a result, John canceled the last few meetings.

John wants to work as equals to accomplish this project on time and to resolve his differences with Amanda. He wants to incorporate both of their ideas. He decides to confront Amanda about his concerns and their differences of opinion.

Question

What difference is at the source of this situation?

Task

How would you respond in this situation? List things that would prevent the situation from escalating into an unpleasant and untenable work situation. Write down what you would say and do to resolve the differences.

Scenario #2

Janet and her co-worker, Becky, have been asked to develop some design training course guidelines. The guidelines should have been completed by Friday, but they missed the deadline. Janet thinks they missed the deadline because Becky canceled the last two meetings. Janet doesn't understand why the meetings were canceled and is upset with Becky for canceling them. Janet feels that Becky is ignoring her.

In addition, Janet is very knowledgeable on the guidelines, but her boss asked her to collaborate on this project with Becky. Janet decides to approach Becky about the canceled meetings and the missed deadline.

Question

What type of difference is at the source of the situation? What strategies do you think would get to the root of the problem?

Task

Identify your ideal response in this situation. How would you go about learning the things you could do to resolve your differences? What would you say to your co-worker?

Scenario #3

Walter wants to take two days off from his job for a religious holiday, which is not recognized as a national or federal holiday. He asks his supervisor for the time off, explaining that it is for religious reasons. She refuses, stating, "We can't spare you at this time. There is too much work to be done."

Walter offers to work on the weekend or during one of the other holidays. His supervisor refuses, stating that one thing has nothing to do with the other.

As a result, Walter feels hurt, angry, and discriminated against for the lack of respect demonstrated toward his culture and religion.

Question

What is the source of this difference? What issue(s) contribute to the difference?

Task

How would you respond? How would you resolve the differences? How many obstacles would you need to overcome before you could resolve the situation? What actions would you take?

Hopefully, from working through these scenarios, you have gained some insight into your own behaviors, as well as those of the other parties involved. As the scenarios demonstrate, differences can evolve into points of disagreement—you may be aware of some points while you may not recognize others. A disagreement continues when differences are not resolved. Your behavior patterns can affect another individual's ability to recognize and work toward resolving the issues stemming from your differences.

Responses to Differences

As a child, you developed your strategies for dealing with differences. Even if your strategies did not resolve differences successfully, you continued to use them because you were unaware of other alternatives. As an adult, you may act in much the same way.

Let's consider some alternatives to your old strategies. First, we will explore how these alternatives are part of a continuum of responses.

Difference-resolution strategies are classified into three categories:

1. Avoidance
2. Diffusion
3. Confrontation

A Continuum of Responses to Difference Situations

Use this diagram as a springboard as you analyze the three categories of difference resolution. While we have discussed various ways to understand differences, a plethora of ways exist in which you can respond to a given situation or problem. You will want to refer back to this avoidance–diffusion–confrontation below, which occurs when differences arise.

Avoidance

Some people attempt to avoid differences or difficult situations altogether. Such people tend to repress emotional reactions, ignore confrontation, or detach from the situation entirely (e.g., quit a job, drop out of school, or get divorced). These individuals either are unable to confront their antagonists directly or lack the skills to negotiate effectively.

Although avoidance may cover up differences, it does not leave the individual satisfied. Avoiding resolving differences is detrimental to an individual's ability to develop negotiation skills and the self-confidence required to resolve difficult situations.

Diffusion

Essentially delaying actions, diffusion strategies temper situations—at least temporarily. Focusing on minor points, while delaying discussion of the major problem or avoiding clarification of salient issues are examples of avoidance escalated to diffusion. Diffusion can be used to "muddy the waters," which renders confrontation impossible. As with avoidance strategies, diffusion leaves a person dissatisfied, anxious about the future, and lacking in self-confidence.

Confrontation

The third major strategy involves directly confronting others to resolve differences. Confrontation is subdivided into power and negotiation strategies. Power strategies include physical force (e.g., violence), bribery (e.g., money, favors), and punishment (e.g., withholding love, money, or promotion). These tactics are only effective if you have the upper hand in the situation.

Negotiation involves discussion of issues and differences. It requires an understanding of the differences and some give and take. This strategy to resolving differences helps to understand the need to find effective alternatives to old strategies and to deal with differences in a way that does not involve the drawbacks discussed previously.

Behavior Arising from Differences

We resort to various behavioral patterns when confronted with strong differences. Let's explore each pattern to get a better understanding of why we sometimes act the way we do when a conflict arises.

Rationalization: Rationalizations are excuses for an individual's inability to accomplish a specific goal.

Regression: An individual who has not reached his or her fullest level of maturity is unable to integrate various forms of coping mechanisms into his or her life. In such cases, this may result in the individual shutting down emotionally, withdrawing from a situation completely, or resorting to some sort of regressive behavioral pattern learned in childhood.

Fixation: In this form of behavior, the individual emotionally exhibits a repeated behavioral pattern. Each time that person experiences turmoil and differences, he or she acts out the same forms of behavior and expects a different result. Individuals with fixations must learn different methods with which they can deal with situations of difference.

Resignation: Apathy occurs after a period of prolonged frustration. People who have reached this point have typically lost all hope of accomplishing their goals and have withdrawn from the situation completely. This is characteristic of people who find themselves in boring and mundane jobs, with little or no reward satisfaction, where there is virtually no hope for improvement or promotion.

Each of these behavioral patterns plays a major role in the way in which each person handles him- or herself when faced with a difference of opinion. Various patterns of behavior will emerge, depending upon how vested and emotionally involved that person has become in the situation and what level the difference has reached.

As you read the following scenarios, notice how behavior can influence attitudes when differences of opinion are involved.

Scenario #1

A manager is concerned about employee relations. Although she feels this way, she doesn't necessarily want to get involved in a situation involving a disgruntled employee. Her concern is overshadowed by her need to avoid confrontation where she withdraws completely from the situation.

Scenario #2

This manager is also concerned about employee relations, but only to quiet what he perceives to be "the masses." He tells his employees what they can and can't do, without paving the way for any kind of open, give-and-take discussion.

Scenario #3

This manager is also concerned about employee relations. He approaches his employees and says, "Gee, I'm sorry. Do you want to air your feelings?" Unfortunately, when they express their feelings and concerns, he takes no action. In other words, no productivity was achieved through his behavior.

Scenario #4

This manager is concerned about employee relations. She approaches her employees and says, "I've heard about your problems, and I'm sorry. I'd like to allow you to air your grievances and concerns, so we can discuss the situation to move toward a more positive and productive working environment."

As you read through the four scenarios, similar values evoke drastically different behaviors. Similarly, there are various ways to handle these differences. When dealing with differences, think about the results and the effect your decisions will have upon the other people involved. Be sure you are looking at the end result with a qualitative form of reasoning, rather than quantitative. Effective employees adapt their behavior to meet the needs of their colleagues, subordinates, and organization.

Your organization, for example, might achieve its highest productivity at the end of a quarter. But what profit is really to be made if employees are unhappy, resign, and go to work with your competitor?

Summary

The continuum of responses to various situations offers three options to deal with differences: avoidance, diffusion, and confrontation. Behavioral patterns prior to a conflict are crucial to understanding the role you play in resolving existing differences. By being aware of your behavior in difficult situations, you will be better able to resolve differences and disagreements.

Chapter 4 — Unpacking Differences

Chapter 4 discusses how attitudes can influence conflict. By assessing the attitudes an individual or group processes about a potential conflict, and gauging what the stakes are, we can usually predict the other person's or group's behavior, thus preventing (or offsetting) the magnitude and scope of the conflict. This chapter discusses pre-conflict strategies you can immediately apply and techniques you can use to help prevent differences from escalating to a state of conflict.

Pre-Conflict Strategies

We have all seen that when conflicts occur, generally the issues remain unresolved, and the differences between the parties are not properly addressed.

Conflict allows us to learn, progress, and grow. While there is no perfect paradigm for handling conflict, the basic strategy for reducing conflict is to find goals upon which the group can agree and to re-establish valid communication among everyone involved. The objective of the strategy is a resolution that is beneficial for all parties. While conflict can result in a satisfactory resolution, most people find conflict undesirable and difficult to manage.

The following is a paradigm that can help explain how to unpack differences before they become a conflict. Four elements contribute to unpacking differences that create conflict: frustration, conceptualization, behaviors, and outcome.

1. **Frustration**. Frustration occurs when a person feels blocked from satisfying a goal-directed activity or concern. The concern may be clear or only vaguely defined; it may be of critical importance or only incidental to the ultimate goal. But the person feels that someone is getting in his or her way of attaining an objective.

2. **Conceptualization**. Conceptualization involves asking key questions (i.e., What's going on here? Is this good or bad? What's the problem? What issues are at stake?). While some conceptualization may be almost instantaneous, others may develop after considerable thought. Conceptualizations may be very sharp and clear, or they may be fuzzy. Regardless of its inception, conceptualization forms the basis of the individual's reaction to frustration and how he or she will ultimately respond to differences.

3. **Behaviors**. Your behaviors flow out of conceptualizing and strategizing—behaviors set in motion a pattern of interaction between the parties in conflict. In the course of this interaction, how each party conceptualizes the conflict may result in deepening frustration. The longer the pattern continues, the more entrenched the adversaries become in their agendas, and the more divergent differences become. As a result, new frustrations, hostility, and resistance can develop from such situations.

4. **Outcome**. Outcome is the state of affairs that exists when differences are resolved. The outcome may be either positive or negative (e.g., the decisions or actions taken and the feelings involved). If the outcome is negative, it is most likely the result of residual frustration.

Residual frustration can generate new differences and plant the seeds for future conflicts. When this situation occurs, the individual may find him- or herself in a situation where, "The cure is worse than the disease."

Perhaps the most tragic illustration of this principle is seen by reviewing the lack of judgment shown by the diplomats who negotiated the Versailles Treaty following World War I when the German generals surrendered to President Woodrow Wilson's respected "Fourteen Points" document.

You will find it helpful to assess the outcome of a pre-conflict resolution of differences using the following three criteria:

1. Was the quality of the decision or action that resulted creative, realistic, or practical?
2. What was the psychological and physical condition of the differing parties upon resolution of the dispute?
3. What was the quality of the relationship between the differing parties? Was there mutual respect and understanding, and were they willing to work together? Or was there hostility and intent to hurt?

These criteria also need to be reconsidered when determining how to behave when differences are not resolved and a conflict result. The criteria also apply an evaluation of the cost and benefits that may have accrued. The way the parties define the problem will significantly influence the chances for a constructive outcome and the feelings realized during the confrontation.

Pros and Cons of Conflict

Although conflict may inflict destruction and unnecessary costs on individuals and organizations, conflict may also result in the attainment of goals, which enables adversaries to ultimately resolve their differences. Conflict is an engine of evolution that allows you to learn, progress, and grow.

Consider the following assumptions:

1. Conflict is an inevitable and important human process.
2. Conflicts are likely to increase in times of change.
3. Conflicts can have either creative or destructive results.

4. Those who understand the processes and dynamics of conflict are better able to deal with the situation, increasing individuals' chances for creative outcomes while minimizing destructive results.

As we've stated, there is no perfect paradigm for handling conflict. The basic strategy for resolving differences in a pre-conflict state is to find goals upon which the parties can agree, then reestablish valid communication with everyone involved. Pursuing this strategy will help resolve difficult situations and what may initially appear to be unresolvable differences. Taking the initiative and being proactive can resolve or, at the very least, reduce differences before they escalate into conflicts.

Responses to Conflicts

In utopian organizations, differences would never turn into conflicts. Since, however, we do not live or work in a utopian society, the most realistic goal is to minimize our differences and best resolve the conflict before long-term damage occurs.

A manager should emphasize the contributions and interaction between groups and not just the end result (i.e., the goal). This involves developing a reward system and, whenever possible, providing employees with new projects to broaden those employees' growth opportunities. Also, a manager should establish a basis for fostering understanding and goodwill among employees.

Elements of Conflict

In today's world, we all live in a network that is changing: family members, colleagues, friends, and schoolmates. In a majority of these change situations, we can find a way to get along with each other. But sometimes it happens that conflicts occur.

Why do people fight? Why can't we all get along? The answer is, most people engage in conflict over goals they deny are important to them, a perceived goal incompatibility, or an interdependent situation.

Conflict is an expressed struggle that exists between two interdependent parities, and that the situations interfere with each achieving their goals. Conflicts are composed of four components:

1. An expressed struggle exists when two or more people involved perceive a disagreement exists between them, even if not verbalized.

2. A perceived incompatible goal situation occurs when it appears the goals of those involved are mutually exclusive. But that is not always the case, as parties can agree upon mutually satisfying answers.

3. Perception of scarce resources (sometimes actual scarcity) occurs when people believe there are not enough resources, such as time, money, or space.

4. Interdependence, real or perceived, implies that people in conflict are dependent on each other, share resources, and/or have mutual goals or interests.

Conflicts are impossible to avoid; the challenge is to handle them effectively when they occur; for example, reframing goals to resolve incompatibility. We do not support the simple notion that if people work together, they would see that their goals are the same.

Opposing goals are a fact of life. Many times, however, people are convinced that they have opposing goals and cannot agree on anything to pursue together. The answer is to consider the elements of each type of conflict, respect the other's point of view, and communicate honestly.

Positive and Negative Aspects of Conflict Exercise

Directions: Read the questions below and think about situations you have encountered. Doing so will enable you to look at your personal reaction to examine positive and negative conflict.

1. What are some positive results from conflict at:
    a) Work—both to the individual and to the organization?
    b) Home—both to the spouse and the family (i.e., children and relatives)?

2. What are some negative outcomes from conflict at:
    a) Work—both to the individual and to the organization?
    b) Home – both to the spouse and the family (i.e., children and relatives)?

What were your responses? Did you find a common thread? Do you have some preventive measures in mind?

Goals and Conflict

Goals should be high enough to consistently challenge the individual to meet them, but realistic enough to attain. Consider the elements of the following situation, where the established goal caused a conflict.

A managing editor assigned an assistant editor a two-day deadline to review a lengthy manuscript. The assistant editor could not begin work until the managing editor and stakeholders finished reviewing the manuscript.

The assistant editor didn't receive the comments from the managing editor and stakeholders until a half-day before the deadline. Because of the time crunch, the assistant editor went to the managing editor and requested an extension of his deadline. The editor refused his request.

Given the time constraints, it was impossible for the assistant editor to meet his deadline. He felt angry, unwilling, and unmotivated to continue working on the manuscript and resigned from his position. The project was left uncompleted.

Ideally, the managing editor would have managed the differences by realizing that the original goals for the assistant editor were no longer feasible. He would have said, "I realize your time was cut, so you're unable to complete the project. If, however, you can do whatever is feasible by close of business today, I will certainly note your efforts and explain the situation to the editor-in-chief."

Despite the difficulty, this simple gesture of understanding and goodwill probably would have motivated the assistant editor to complete the task. Positive reinforcement, rather than punishment, would have helped the employee to achieve the senior editor's goal.

Negative and Positive Outcomes of Conflict

The following are negative outcomes of conflict:

- Debilitation
- Distraction from achieving your goals
- Defensiveness and rigidity
- Distortion of reality
- Negative cycles
- Escalation and proliferation of additional conflicting issues.

These are positive outcomes of conflict:

- Increased motivation and energy

- Clarification of issues and positions

- Building of self and group awareness

- Results that lead to innovation and creativity

- Creation of better interpersonal relationships.

Win-Lose, Lose-Lose, or Win-Win

Due to a misunderstanding or lack of communication at the outset, differences among partners frequently result in conflict. If and when a conflict arises, it's important to know that there are three stages of conflict. As you will see, some stages can yield positive results, while others may prove detrimental to all parties.

"I win–you lose" occurs when conflict is inevitable and agreement becomes impossible. In simplistic terms, this comes down to the "somebody's going to win, somebody's going to lose" power struggle. In this situation, when an individual believes agreement is impossible, behavior will range from passive to active. If the stakes are low, the individual may be passive enough to let fate decide the outcome of the conflict.

When the stakes are moderate, a third party may be called upon to decide the outcome of the conflict. When, however, the stakes are riding high, the situation deteriorates. At this point, individuals will actively engage in an "I win–you lose" power struggle, which results in only one perceived winner.

"Lose–lose" presents itself when a conflict may not be prevented—when stakes are high, and both parties are emotionally involved. In this instance, people will eventually isolate themselves from the situation at hand, with both parties ultimately withdrawing into their corners.

"Win–win" conflicts can be detected early on in a conflict. This situation makes it possible for intervention to occur. In addition in "win–win" situations, the stakes are lowered to permit mediation by a neutral third party. This kind of mediation can aid in the belief that agreement is possible even though a conflict exists. Because of the behavior that occurs in this stage of conflict, "win–win" situations are known for being action-oriented, enabling an individual to move toward an active problem-solving mode.

As you can see, very real, negative consequences may result from mismanagement and misunderstanding. Such situations can be debilitating and can distract from achieving your goals. Conflict can contribute to the increased defensiveness and rigidity of everyone involved. It can distort reality, contribute to a negatively reinforcing cycle, escalate or make the situation more egregious, and generate additional issues that will require resolution.

If you can accurately assess the attitudes an individual or group possesses about potential conflict and gauge what the stakes are, you can most often predict the other person's or the group's behavior (and vice-versa).

Summary

Conflicts can occur when differences are not properly managed or resolved. When this happens, the parties view one another as the enemy. As hostility between individuals increases, communication ceases to function, and differences can become completely unresolvable. Thus, you must learn to unpack or to assess the situation.

In the unpacking process, you effectively use communication tools to resolve differences and disagreements. The way the parties define the problem greatly influences the chances for a constructive outcome.

By assessing the attitudes an individual or group possesses about a potential conflict, and gauging what the stakes are, we can usually predict the other person's or the group's behavior, thus preventing (or offsetting) the magnitude and scope of the conflict. Using these techniques can help prevent differences from escalating to a state of conflict.

Chapter 5 — Managing Differences

Most people view differences in a negative light—something bad that must be avoided, minimized, or eliminated. Differences can also be viewed positively, as opportunities for learning and growth and for developing new social skills that can help a person communicate more effectively.

Left unmanaged, differences can drain creativity and energy. Managing differences effectively will help minimize a potentially negative outcome and maximize the opportunities to attain desired goals.

The focus of this book is to provide guidance to manage and resolve personal and professional differences skillfully.

Identifying the various sources of differences is the first step in learning how effectively to manage disagreements and ultimately to work toward a resolution. The second step you need is to identify how we have typically managed differences, which is an individual's preferred style.

Identifying Styles of Managing Differences

Most likely, you learned your preferred method of handling differences during your childhood. Your inherently unique style has been influenced by your upbringing, your experiences, and the world around you.

This questionnaire is designed to give you information about your preferred method of dealing with differences. Once you know your style, you can analyze your preferred method and assess its value to you.

The style that you'll determine from the questionnaire only indicates your preferred style. No style is set in stone. While you might have a predominant style in various situations (e.g., in personal relationships), your style will change in other circumstances (e.g., in high-pressured, work-related situations).

Managing Differences Styles Questionnaire

Directions: Each statement below provides a strategy for dealing with conflict. Rate each statement on a scale from 1 to 4 indicating how likely you would be to use the strategy.

1 = Rarely   2 = Sometimes   3 = Often   4 = Always

1. I explore issues with others to find solutions that meet everyone's needs.
2. I try to negotiate and adopt a give-and-take approach to problem situations.
3. I try to meet the expectations of others.
4. I would argue my case and insist on the merits of my point of view.
5. Where there is a disagreement, I gather information and share openly.
6. When in an argument, I usually say very little and leave as soon as possible.
7. I try to see conflict from both sides. What do I/they need? What's the issue?
8. I prefer to compromise when solving problems and just move on.
9. I find conflicts challenging and exhilarating; I enjoy battles.
10. Being at odds with people makes me feel uncomfortable and anxious.
11. I try to accommodate the wishes of my friends and family.
12. I can figure out what needs to be done, and I am usually right.
13. To break deadlocks, I would meet people halfway.
14. I may not get what I want, but it's a small price to pay for keeping the peace.
15. I avoid hard feelings by keeping my disagreements with others to myself.

Scoring

The 15 statements correspond to the five conflict resolution styles. To identify your most preferred style, total the points in each of the categories. The category with the highest score indicates your most commonly used strategy. The one with the lowest score indicates your least preferred style.

Styles Corresponding Statements Total

- Competing: 4, 9, 12 _______
- Accommodation: 3, 11, 14 _______
- Avoiding: 6, 10, 15 _______
- Compromising: 2, 8, 13 _______
- Collaborating: 1, 5, 7 _______

Style Descriptors

Five styles are appropriate for managing differences: competition, accommodation, avoidance, compromise, and collaboration. All of the styles have their strengths. Understanding your style is the key to handling a given situation.

Competing Style: Authoritarian approach.

Competition is a power-oriented, win-lose approach. You use whatever power you have available to win, forcing the other party to concede his or her differences.

- Pros: Goal-oriented; quick.
- Cons: May breed hostility.

Accommodation Style: Giving in to maintain relationships.

Accommodation is the opposite of competition. When accommodating, you neglect your own differences and yield to those of the other person.

- Pros: Minimizes injury when we are outmatched; relationships are maintained.

- Cons: Breeds resentment; exploits weak.

Avoiding Style: The non-confrontational approach.

Avoidance is side-stepping or, at least, postponing the airing of any differences. By avoidance, consciously or subconsciously you choose not to resolve any difference. In this way, you avoid a confrontation.

- Pros: Does not escalate conflict; postpones difficulty.

- Cons: Unaddressed problems; unresolved problems.

Compromising Style: Middle group approach.

Compromise is splitting the difference, giving a little and taking a little, seeking a middle ground. Compromise falls somewhere in between competition and collaboration. Both parties get some, but not all, of what they want.

- Pros: Useful in complex issues without simple solutions; all parties are equal in power.

- Cons: No one is ever really satisfied; less than optimal solutions get implemented.

Collaborating Style: Win-win.

Problems are solved in ways that provide an optimum result for all involved. Both sides get what they want, and negative feelings are minimized.

Collaboration is win–win, aimed at finding the best possible solution, using all available ideas and resources that fully satisfy the needs of both parties. Both parties should try to identify their underlying concerns and differences and to find alternatives that meet everyone's needs.

- Pros: Creates mutual trust; maintains positive relationships; builds commitments.

- Cons: Time consuming; energy consuming.

Your Score

When it comes to behaviors that manage differences, there are no right or wrong answers. All five styles are useful in certain situations; each represents a distinct set of useful social skills. It's important that we learn how to work through our patterns so that we can use the style most appropriate for a situation. Consider the following:

- How surprised are you about your preferred style?
- What did you learn about your preferred style for handling differences?
- What are the strengths of your style?
- What are the drawbacks of your preferred style?
- How does your score differ from your prediction?
- What strengths of your style can help you deal effectively with differences in your relationships?
- What areas of your style require improvement for you to effectively manage differences in your relationships?
- How does the chart match your job role?
- What risks are involved with using your style at your job?
- What are your strengths in dealing with the differences between others at your workplace?
- What areas can you improve upon in dealing with differences in your workplace?

Things to keep in mind as you work through differences:

- There are almost always differences in viewpoint between two or more individual parties over a given issue at any point in time.
- Differences become apparent when multiple parties are concerned about turf, resources, rewards, functions, and technical issues.

- Differences are inevitable.

- Differing viewpoints are useful and necessary for creativity.

- Differences can lead to either competition or collaboration.

The reward structure that is in place in any social situation provides the incentive for the differences to result in a productive or destructive situation. If only limited reward is available, one person is forced to win, and the other must lose; the situation will become competitive. However, if it is possible for all parties involved to achieve their goals, and the achievement of one person's goals involves or leads to goal achievement by another, the situation is collaborative.

It's not hard to think of examples of pure competitive and collaborative situations. A serious tennis game or the interaction between a prospective car buyer and a used car dealer are purely competitive situations.

Managing Behavior

The first step in managing a competitive situation is to identify the source of the difference. The behaviors most appropriate and effective in a competitive situation are quite different from, and often directly opposite from behaviors that are most effective in a collaborative situation. Following is a partial list of behaviors or strategies appropriate and effective in competitive situations.

Competitive Behavior:

- Behavior is directed toward achieving personal goals.

- The parties make sure the opponents don't know the differences and goals they want to achieve.

- While accurately understanding one's own needs and differences, the parties keep them either hidden or misrepresented. If others do not know exactly what an individual wants and how much he or she wants it, they don't know what that person is willing to give up to get it.

- Unpredictable, mixed strategies use the element of surprise.
- The parties use threats and bluffs to take each other by surprise.
- Illogical or irrational arguments are used to defend a position to which the parties are strategically committed.
- When teams, committees, or organizations are involved, each group communicates negative stereotypes of the other group, ignoring logic and convincing others they mean business.

Guiding Effective Collaborative Behavior

Collaborative behavior is defined as working together to achieve a common goal. When differences might occur, share your point of view or difference and work to achieve a resolution that both parties can accept. Here are seven guiding principles commonly used to help one understand and manage a difference:

1. Behavior is directed toward resolving differences and, ultimately, achieving common goals.
2. Parties are open in discussing, settling, and resolving differences.
3. The parties understand and accurately represent their needs and differences.
4. Although flexible behavior is appropriate, it is not designed to take the other party by surprise.
5. Threats and bluffs are not used to take the other person by surprise.
6. Parties use logical and innovative processes to defend their views and to settle differences—when they are convinced the viewpoints are valid—or try to find solutions to problems.
7. Success demands that stereotypes are dropped, that differences are openly discussed, and that all ideas are given consideration on their merit. Good working relationships

are maintained. Positive feelings about others are both a cause and an effect of collaboration.

Most of the social and professional situations in which we find ourselves are neither purely competitive nor purely collaborative. One complication is that, by default, we all must play the competitive and collaborative games simultaneously. This occurs most commonly when we try to problem-solve with the same persons with whom we are competing for promotions or when workgroups are vying for the highest performance ratings and must also work together to complete an assignment.

The cynic approaches every situation as if it were a competitive game, transforming every discussion into a debate. A naive individual may be in danger of approaching every situation as if it were a collaborative game. The realist may recognize the objective reality of the situation and choose dual approaches that are appropriate for the coexisting conditions.

The common problem in the workplace today is cynicism. We characteristically approach situations as if they were competitive games when, in fact, they are not. In the early decades of industrialization, worker-management relations were conducted in a strictly win-lose style, as if the entire process were competitive bargaining (i.e., what the workers gained, management lost, and vice versa). Attitudes do shift over time, and parties now realize that a more collaborative approach to managing oneself and others achieves better results.

Attitudinal change is key to the use of collaborative behavior as a substitute for competitive behavior to resolve differences. Parties need to begin to know each other and to regard one another with some measure of trust. Establishing trust allows us to achieve the harmony that leads to the mutual respect of each party's differences. Then the parties can begin to examine the situation to find its collaborative aspects.

Now let's continue to explore the different characteristics and facets of collaborative and competitive behaviors.

Collaboration

1. Win–win
2. Flexible
3. Make concessions in turn
4. Ask questions and explore positions
5. Usually interested in the other party's needs

Competition

1. Win–lose
2. Adversarial
3. Inflexible
4. No concessions
5. Don't ask questions or explore positions
6. Not interested in the other party's needs

Conflict Style Action Plan

Now that you've learned about managing differences and some strategies that enable you to resolve differences collaboratively, you can begin to capitalize on what you've learned by completing the following action plan.

1. The three most important things I learned about managing differences are:

    a.

    b.

    c.

2. In light of Item 1, I plan to take the following three actions more often:

    a.

    b.

    c.

3. In light of Item 1, I plan to do the following less often:

    a.

    b.

    c.

4. The three obstacles to accomplishing these changes are:

    a.

    b.

    c.

Summary

After exploring the various aspects of collaborative and competitive behavior, does it surprise you to learn that collaboration is the best strategy to use to manage differences? Unfortunately, in many situations, you may not have the opportunity to use purely collaborative behaviors to resolve differences. In those cases, you can still work toward a positive resolution of differences. Just recognize that competitive behaviors will affect your ability to achieve your goals.

Chapter 6 — The Intricacies of Managing Differences

You have developed skills designed to help you manage differences. Our final focus will be on some of the intricacies that can develop during that managing process. This additional knowledge will be helpful, especially when dealing with differences in more difficult situations.

That's because differences can be categorized as one of two types. There are real differences, which are based on tangible evidence, and there are value differences, which are based on an ideology.

Four Skills

Did you know that nearly 70 percent of U.S. cities fluoridate their drinking water? Yet for many years, there were significant real differences as to whether fluoridation was beneficial. The differences were based on measurable facts. Another example: for years, women in Saudi Arabia were not allowed to drive automobiles. That ban was an ideological one. Recently the ban was lifted partly because of tangible benefits, e.g., women having access to driving may increase their participation in the workplace and thus help the country's economy.

Because of these two types of differences, managing them requires learning a particular set of skills. These skills include a person's

- ability to diagnose the types of differences
- effectiveness at initiating a discussion
- listening to others point of view
- use of the problem-solving process to reach an amicable resolution.

Diagnose

Real differences can be measurable and thus more capable of resolutions. Ideological differences can be more difficult because of a lack of tangible proof. You need to identify the type of difference before trying to initiate a discussion, let alone attempt a resolution. Bear in mind that ideological differences cannot always be resolved.

Initiate

It is essential to initiate a conversation with the other party to have any chance of resolving differences. Note that you need to start a conversation, not a confrontation. Confrontation will only create a stumbling block to reaching a resolution.

Let's take one initiation as an example. A staff member approaches her supervisor and says, "I have a problem. Due to your stance on overnight travel, I'm unable to apply for the supervisory position that I feel I'm qualified to handle." This is a more effective approach to initiating a conversation than saying, "You're discriminating against me because of my child care responsibilities."

Notice that the first—and more polite—initiation is based upon facts. The policy on overnight travel is not only real; it's probably a written rule. That's tangible! How and when the policy may change is not the purpose of this discussion, but how to properly initiate is. Next is listening.

Listen

The person above politely initiated a conversation. They stated their concern, and now it is time to let the other side speak while they listen. Defensive rebuttals can ensue when the initial statement made by one person is not what the other person was hoping to hear. Therefore, avoid any replies that may provoke an argument. And do not attempt to defend yourself, explain your position, or make demands or threats. Instead, engage in active listening by paraphrasing or clarifying the other person's position. Only after you've interpreted the opposition's point of view in a manner that is satisfactory to them should you state your point of view.

Problem Solve

The fourth skill needed to resolve differences is problem-solving. There are five steps in the problem-solving process. They are basic and easy to apply.

1. Clarify the problem. What is the tangible difference? Where does each party stand on the issue? In the example above, the initiator believes a one-sided policy is stymieing her career advancement. Her supervisor may only be following rules set by a superior.

2. Generate and evaluate possible solutions. Often steps 1 and 2 should be taken exclusive of each other. First, raise all possible differences, brainstorm for solutions to each difference, and only then evaluate each proposed solution.

3. Decide together on what is the best solution, and that is usually the solution most acceptable to all parties.

4. Plan the implementation of the solution, including how and when it will be implemented.

5. Plan for an evaluation of the solution after a specific period of time. This step is essential because the first solution chosen may not always be the best or the most workable. If that is the case, then you need to repeat the five steps.

Together these five steps are effective tactics for managing real or ideological differences. These are the basic skills to help you achieve meaningful resolution of differences.

Signals and Emotions

Having stated that the five problem-solving steps are key to resolving differences, you should also be aware that there can be signals that indicate a difference between yourself and others. Some signals are visceral, while others are intuitive.

For example, emotions can play a powerful role in some situations. Some people take great pains to hide their fear, anger, or depression. Others can let their emotions run rampant, and a heated debate result. In such situations, coping with the key issues of a difference can be difficult, if not impossible.

When you know when, what, or who affects you emotionally, you'll be better able to recognize and confront not only your anger and emotional outbursts but also those of others.

Four elements provide guidance when dealing with emotional situations.

Dealing with Emotional Situations

Four basic elements provide excellent guidance when the discussion about differences escalates to an emotional level.

1. *Separate the people from the problem.* When people and problems meld, emotions become entangled with resolving the problem. Taking and holding a position while refusing to settle the differences makes a situation worse. To resolve their differences, people must come to see themselves as working side-by-side to attack the problem and not each other.

2. *Focus on interests, not on positions.* Your position can often obscure what you want. Hiding your true interests to maintain a particular position is not likely to produce an effective resolution to your differences or a lasting agreement from either party.

3. *Invent options for mutual gain.* Free yourself from constraints that prevent you from reaching optimal solutions. These may be organizational or personal. Instead, set

aside a designated period of time to discuss your differences. Create a range of possible solutions designed to advance the group's shared interests while reconciling the disputed issues.

4. *Insist on using objective criteria.* Establish a fair standard to evaluate your decisions, independent of anyone's will. Avoid defensive positions stating what you are willing or unwilling to do. Objective criteria will encourage all parties to reach an equitable solution.

While these four elements provide tactics for managing differences, one vital element can help both sides manage their difference— negotiation. The chief objective of negotiation is to resolve differences through compromise or to find a satisfying solution for all involved parties. Negotiation provides the most positive and least negative results of all strategies aimed at managing differences.

Negotiating to Win

According to Roger Fisher in *Getting to Yes: Negotiating Agreement Without Giving In* (2011), the definition of negotiation is "the reaching of agreement through discussion and compromise." Negotiation, when applied appropriately, is a powerful and invaluable tool in mediating, managing, and resolving differences. When presenting your ideas to an opposing party, you can use negotiation to influence, convince, and persuade.

Negotiating Persuasively

To develop negotiating skills, you need to assume the role of the negotiator. Seven basic principles can help you achieve negotiator status.

1. *Trustworthiness.* Do people view you as credible? Can an opponent sense that you are confident and display good qualities, especially fairness, truth, honor, or ability?

2. *Expertise.* This relates to informational power. Are you perceived as an expert, as a person who possesses certain information that is of value or is highly integral to the issue at hand? If so, you may hold the upper hand in the negotiation process.

3. *Dynamism.* Are you perceived as dynamic in both your personal and professional lives? People like being around those who inspire enthusiasm, interest, or affection in others through personal charm or influence.

4. *Sympathy.* Can you be sympathetic to another person's point of view? Sympathy does not require you to make an exaggerated show of emotions. But it does require an earnest attempt to understand the differences, views, and positions held by others.

5. *Power.* Personal power is a source of influence and authority a person has over his or her followers. And in short, one's power is determined by his or her followers.

6. *Idealism.* An idealist is a person who seeks to get the best from a situation. An idealist contributes his or her ideas in a manner that is perceived as positive by others. Using the seven principles when negotiating, idealism can be useful to defuse a situation or to mediate with all parties in a dispute.

7. *Goodwill.* Men and women of goodwill express genuine concern for the welfare and wellbeing of others. They are perceived as wanting others to succeed in their endeavors.

These seven personal principles are important in the negotiation process. Each principle can be a powerful bargaining chip. Next we will discuss how to use those skills with strategies for effective negotiation.

Negotiating Effectively

Successful negotiation requires a combination of the principles of persuasion and effective behavior patterns. By assessing a situation, you will be able to gauge which of these principles would be the most beneficial to you as a negotiator. And it is equally important to develop a strategic plan for approaching your differences with a specific individual or group.

We'll use the example of buying a car to demonstrate the 10 strategies that you can use to create a winning behavior plan.

1. *Do your homework.* Always attempt to negotiate differences armed with knowledge. If you have to be armed at all, this is most likely the most positive contribution you can make. Stephen Covey, author of the *7 Habits of Highly Effective People* (2004), puts it plainly, "Seek first to understand, then to be understood." In addition to practical demographic information, this means doing your best to avoid stereotypes and to demonstrate that you are interested in exploring creative solutions.

2. *Everything is negotiable.* Most negotiators start with an ideal, or even an "in your dreams," objective. Smart negotiators recognize that this ideal is not their true goal. The real goal is to find a solution acceptable to all parties involved. When purchasing a car, this means identifying a price the buyer will pay, that the bank will authorize for a loan, which the sales manager will accept so that the salesperson can make their sales commission.

3. *Never pay the sticker price.* Since everything is negotiable, the sticker price is only the car company's ideal price and its first bid. In some cases, the sticker price only indicates the maximum amount the car dealer can sell the car for and remain competitive.

4. *Bid low and haggle.* This is your opportunity to let the salesperson know your dream goal.

5. *Don't commit yourself to anything.* Negotiation is only talking. It's the opportunity to explore options.

6. *Start slowly and be patient.* If you are in too much of a hurry, you probably will not find a solution that satisfies all the parties.

7. *Crunch early and often.* Crunching is the judicious application of pressure, telling the other party you are not satisfied with their offer. For example, when the salesperson writes out a price proposal for the car that you think is too high, you may crunch by saying, "I think you need to sharpen your pencil."

8. *Make smaller concessions, especially toward the end.* As you get nearer to an acceptable offer, preserve your resources.

9. *Keep looking for alternatives.* Creative solutions are seldom the first things we suggest. Some solutions won't even occur to you until you begin to talk and brainstorm.

10. *Leave your opponent feeling that they have done well.* Anyone who leaves a negotiation feeling negatively will be back, perhaps with a vengeance.

Summary

These are the bare essentials to managing differences, from identifying whether they are tangible or not, to diagnosis and initiation, listening, and problem-solving. Then we addressed dealing with emotional situations, principles of persuasive negation, and lastly, strategies for effective negotiation.

Conclusion

This book has provided you with a number of ways to handle difficult situations effectively. Awareness, willingness, logic, and creativity combined with good listening skills will help you on your journey to becoming an effective manager and mediator of the variety of conflicts based on differences that are inevitable in today's homes and workplaces.

Be creative in your method of handling, managing, and resolving differences. Don't allow your differences to result in a passionate debate in which you become driven by emotions. An emotional rollercoaster makes you unable to think clearly or use logical strategies to resolve your differences. That creates undue tension and communication breakdowns. If communication does break down, all parties must walk away from the table and resolve any anger or defensiveness before resuming negotiations.

The most vital ingredient in resolving differences is your ability to negotiate. Remember that during the pre-conflict stage, different viewpoints can be most easily discussed, understood, and ultimately incorporated into both your personal and professional life. When you address differences properly at the outset, you will successfully avoid nonproductive conflict.

The seven principles to successful negotiation (trustworthiness, expertise, dynamism, sympathy, power, idealism, and goodwill), combined with an effective persuasion strategy and consideration for the individual's true needs, are your most powerful tools to help everyone involved in a dispute over differences to walk away feeling like a winner!